For Marlene, Doug, Cindy, and Dave
—A. P. S.

For Robin
—S. J.

For scientific review, thank you to Steven M. Sullivan, curator of Urban Ecology at the Chicago Academy of Sciences and Petty Notebaert Nature Museum; John L. Koprowski, professor of Wildlife Conservation at the University of Arizona; Etienne Benson, assistant professor at the University of Pennsylvania; and Jeff Sayre, coauthor of the *Kaufman Field Guide to Nature of the Midwest*. My thanks to fellow authors JoAnn Early Macken, Phyllis Harris, Carolyn Crimi, and Gretchen Woelfle. Gratitude to Mumsie and ocean/treetop explorer Liz Cunningham, author of *Ocean Country*. Thanks also to Almond and the Sideways Squirrel.

Henry Holt and Company, LLC
Publishers since 1866
175 Fifth Avenue
New York, New York 10010
mackids.com

Henry Holt® is a registered trademark of Henry Holt and Company, LLC.
Text copyright © 2016 by April Pulley Sayre
Illustrations copyright © 2016 by Steve Jenkins
All rights reserved.

Library of Congress Cataloging-in-Publication Data
Names: Sayre, April Pulley, author. | Jenkins, Steve, 1952– illustrator.
Title: Squirrels leap, squirrels sleep / April Pulley Sayre ; illustrated by Steve Jenkins.
Description: New York : Henry Holt and Company, [2016] | Audience: Ages 4–8.
Identifiers: LCCN 2015036529 | ISBN 9780805092516 (hardcover)
Subjects: LCSH: Squirrels—Juvenile literature.
Classification: LCC QL737.R68 S25 2016 | DDC 599.36—dc23
LC record available at http://lccn.loc.gov/2015036529

Our books may be purchased in bulk for promotional, educational, or business use.
Please contact your local bookseller or the Macmillan Corporate and Premium Sales Department at
(800) 221-7945 ext. 5442 or by e-mail at MacmillanSpecialMarkets@macmillan.com.

First Edition—2016
Book design by Anna Booth
The artist used cut- and torn-paper collage to create the illustrations for this book.
Printed in China by Toppan Leefung Printing Ltd., Dongguan City, Guangdong Province

3 5 7 9 10 8 6 4

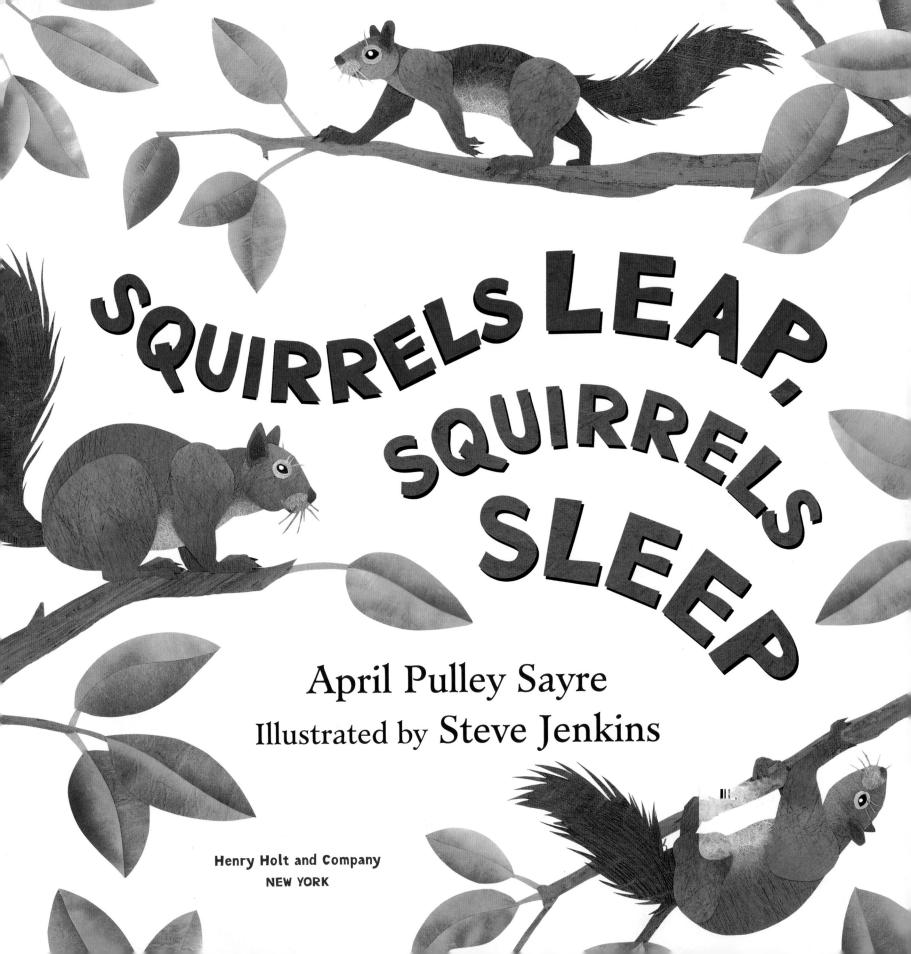

SQUIRRELS LEAP, SQUIRRELS SLEEP

April Pulley Sayre

Illustrated by Steve Jenkins

Henry Holt and Company
NEW YORK

Squirrels wrestle.
Squirrels leap.
Squirrels climb.
Squirrels sleep.

Meet the squirrels:
Gray. Fox. Red.
Flying squirrel
overhead.

Tail umbrella.
Tail as flag.
Tail for balance,
zig and zag!

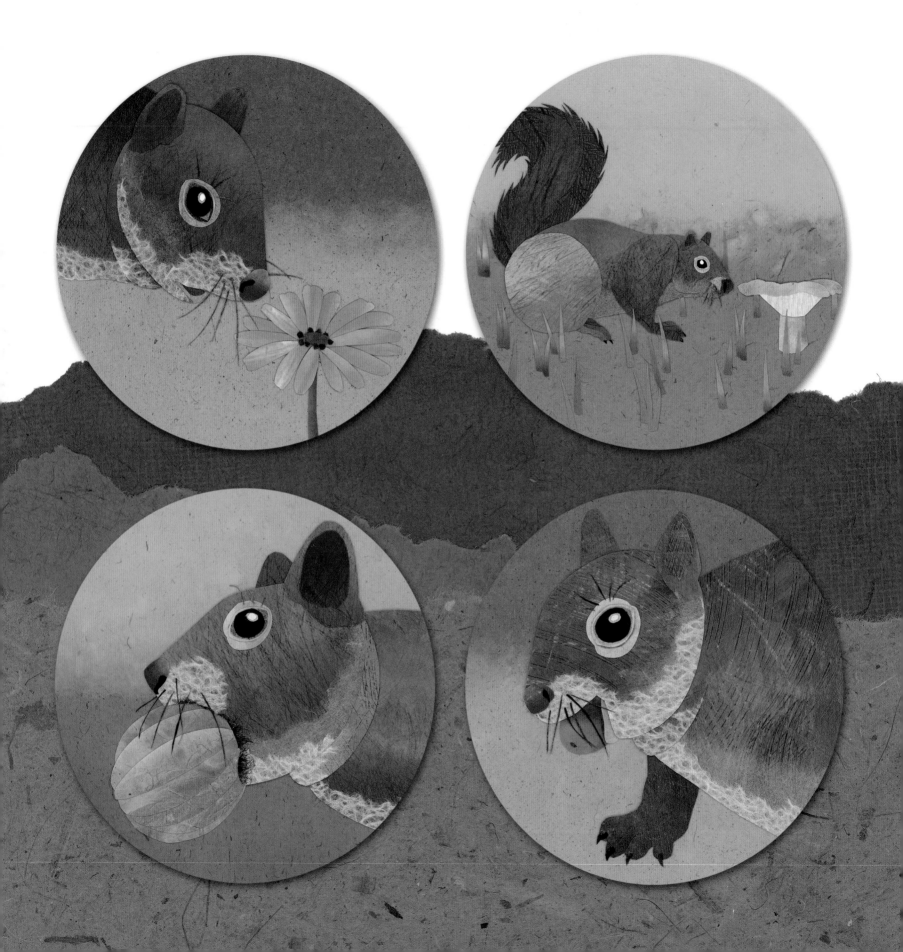

Nose for sniffing.
Jaws to chew.
Eyes for looking
back at you.

Paws for climbing.
Paws to pick.
Paws for cleaning.
Paws run. Quick!

Squirrels chirp.
Squirrels drink.
Can you guess
what squirrels think?

Squirrels reach.
Squirrels rest
in a tree hole
or a nest.

Squirrels gather.
Squirrels store.
How many seeds?
More, more, more!

Squirrels stretch.
Squirrels yawn.
Munch the acorns.
Are they gone?

Five are hidden.
Will they sprout?

Seedlings push
up, up, and out!

Trunks grow upward.
Trunks grow wide.
Squirrels circle.
Squirrels hide.

Squirrels wrestle.
Squirrels leap.
Squirrels climb.
And…

...squirrels sleep.

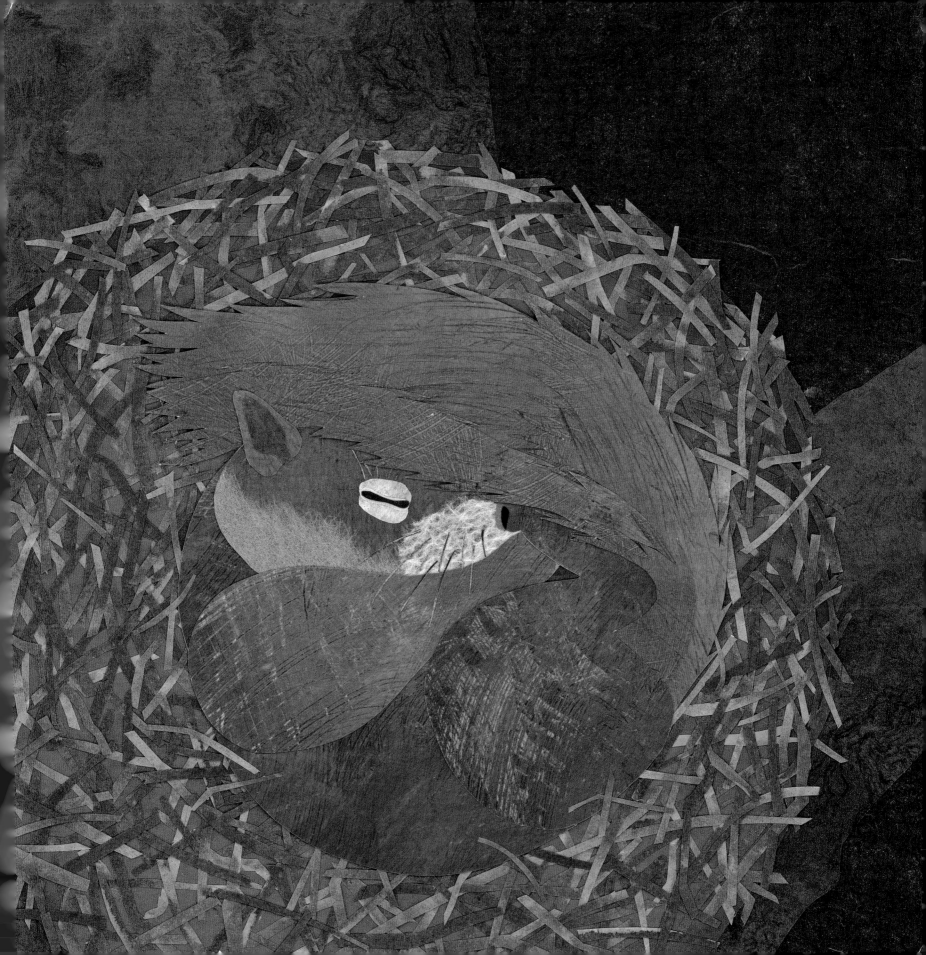

SQUIRRELS AND THEIR TREES

Species in This Book

The eastern fox squirrel (*Sciurus niger*) is the largest tree squirrel native to North America. The natural range of the fox squirrel overlaps with the eastern gray squirrel (*Sciurus carolinensis*) and American red squirrel (*Tamiasciurus hudsonicus*), which are also in this book's illustrations.

Although northern and southern flying squirrels live in the same forests as fox, gray, and red squirrels, they rarely cross paths. Flying squirrels are nocturnal—active at night—and the other squirrels are active during the day.

Tails As Tools

A squirrel's tail helps the squirrel balance. A squirrel can stretch or curl its tail to distribute body weight as it climbs. A squirrel may also curl its tail over its head when it rains, helping to keep water off the rest of its body. (This works in light rain, but heavy rain can soak the squirrel.) Many squirrels also communicate with one another by waving their tails.

Squirrels Glide

Fox, gray, or red squirrels can jump a long way, but they cannot glide like flying squirrels. A flying squirrel leaps from a high perch. It spreads its limbs. Stretched between the front and back limbs is a *patagium*—a wide flap of skin that acts like a kite. Using this patagium, a flying squirrel can glide a distance of almost 200 feet (61 meters). Is gliding the same as flying? Some people say yes. Others say no because gliding does not involve flapping.

Early Life

Fox and gray squirrels tend to be born in either February–March or June–July. At birth, fox and gray squirrels are hairless and pink. They cannot see or hear. At three weeks, their ears open. At four to five weeks, their eyes open. At seven to eight weeks old, they leave the nest for the first time. But they remain in the tree near the nest for several more days.

Feeding Time

A newborn squirrel's first food is its mother's milk. After three months, it must begin to find its own food. Squirrels gather seeds such as maple seeds, hickory nuts, and acorns. They also eat berries and buds. Squirrels find food not just by sight but also by smell. They use their noses to locate mushrooms, nuts, and roots.

All in the Family

Squirrels are rodents, a type of mammal. (Other rodents include beavers, capybaras, mice, rats, prairie dogs, and porcupines.) The word *rodent* comes from the Latin word *rodere*, which means "to gnaw." Rodents have two large front teeth called incisors. Gnawing helps wear down the incisors. If

...ts don't chew hard foods, these teeth can grow ...o long for their mouths. (Humans have incisors, too. Fortunately, human incisors do not continue growing throughout life as rodents' teeth do.)

Within the order Rodentia (rodents), squirrels belong to the family Sciuridae. Woodchucks, prairie dogs, and chipmunks are in this family as well. Of the world's 285 Sciuridae species, 66 live in the United States and Canada.

Both fox squirrels and gray squirrels vary in fur color. Gray squirrels, despite their name, can also be all white or all black in color. Fox squirrels are typically reddish brown but can also be black with white ears and a white belly.

Tree Hole Homes

Fox, gray, red, and flying squirrels are usually born in tree holes called cavities. These tree cavities often start as woodpecker homes. A woodpecker excavates a tree hole and uses it as a nest. The next year, it makes a new tree cavity. (See our book *Woodpecker Wham!* for more about the lives of these important home builders.) The squirrel moves into the hole left empty by the woodpecker. The squirrel may renovate by chewing the entrance hole and wall to enlarge the cavity. It lines the tree cavity with leaves.

Squirrels also make nests of leaves up on tree branches. A squirrel may build several nests and nap in any of them. If you see a squirrel carrying rolled leaves in its mouth, it is likely working on one of its leaf nests or freshening the lining of its tree cavity. Squirrels may also raise their families entirely in leaf nests, especially if tree cavities are not plentiful in the area.

Squirrels: The Planters

In fall, fox squirrels and gray squirrels spend a lot of time on the ground gathering oak seeds, called acorns. (They also gather hickory nuts, beechnuts, and other tree nuts.) Squirrels do not automatically eat every acorn. They inspect acorns for holes and rotten spots. They eat and bury only the fresher ones. Eastern oak tree species fall into two main groups: white and red. Squirrels tend to eat white oak acorns right away and store red oak acorns for later. Red oak acorns last better in storage. Many buried acorns are never eaten. Some of those acorns sprout. They may grow to become trees.

Overwhelmed by Acorns

Every three to twelve years, oaks have a mast year. In a mast year, all the nearby trees of the same oak species produce more acorns than in a regular year. The local animals cannot eat all these acorns. This helps the trees because more acorns survive to sprout and grow.

During mast years, plentiful acorns help more squirrels to survive. In the year after a mast year, however, there are many squirrels but just the usual number of acorns. So some squirrels may go hungry. Historical records tell of mass movements of millions of gray squirrels in September of these years.

Conifer Seed Collectors

American red squirrels belong to a group of squirrels commonly known as pine squirrels. Pine squirrels often live in conifers—trees that produce seeds inside cones. (Douglas's squirrels, or chickarees, found in the western United States, are a type of red squirrel.) Like many wild animals, red squirrels hoard food. They save it for times when food is scarce. Red squirrels often pile hundreds of seed-filled cones in storage sites called middens. Bears sometimes dig up these middens and steal the seeds. (You can find an illustration of this in our book *Eat Like a Bear*.) In contrast, fox squirrels and gray squirrels are considered scatter hoarders because they store seeds by stashing them in scattered locations, instead of in a few big piles.

Squirrel Ancestors

A white oak tree in a city neighborhood can easily be 150 years old. A wild gray or fox squirrel can live for about eight years. So squirrels are born and live in oaks that may have been planted by their great-great-great-great-great-great-great-great-great-great-great-great-great-great-great-grandfather or -grandmother squirrels.

Long-lived trees such as oak, hickory, and beech are very important to squirrels and other wildlife. They do more than produce seeds that animals eat. Woodpeckers, bees, raccoons, possums, and birds also make homes on and inside these trees.

Helping Oaks and Animals

Trees are the best bird and squirrel houses and feeders you can provide. They are likely to last longer and help more animals than anything made with a saw and hammer. So—plant a tree!

Ask the naturalist at a local nature center about what trees are native to your area. Plant trees that provide food for wildlife. Be sure to plant some large, long-lived trees, such as oak or hickory. They will make the biggest impact. Up in the air, a large tree provides a huge area of wildlife habitat among its branches. Remember, trees will grow LARGE, so think about their future size when you decide where to plant them.

If there are already oak or hickory trees in your area, look for seedlings sprouting and growing. Ask family, friends, and any landowners to let some of these trees grow! Perhaps you can help build a flower bed or set rocks or other markers around a growing oak tree to protect it. Food and water travel through a tree's bark, so it's important not to let lawn mowers scrape too close to a tree.

You could also transplant a tree. Just make sure it is a very young tree, because many trees have a taproot—an extremely long, central root that is crucial to the tree's survival. If the taproot breaks, the tree is less likely to survive. It's a good idea to transplant several trees at once. Some will likely die, but a few should grow and thrive.

Often, the soil conservation service or department of wildlife will provide trees for free or at low cost. To find trees, contact these departments, as well as nature centers and plant nurseries.

Old Tree Neighborhoods

Look around your town. Are there any young trees growing? Some neighborhoods have big, old trees. But often people forget to plant new trees or to let young trees mature. The time to start young trees growing is *before* the biggest, oldest ones fall down. A young tree does not produce enough acorns or nesting sites to help many animals. It needs time to mature. So think ahead—far ahead. Consider squirrels and birds that will live in your neighborhood in the future. Perhaps you can create a "tree team" to help neighbors who need a hand doing the work of planting trees. Not only will you make a neighbor happy, you will help squirrels, too.

Further Reading

Bowers, Nora, Rick Bowers, and Kenn Kaufman. *Kaufman Field Guide to Mammals of North America.* Boston: Houghton Mifflin Co., 2007.

Hartson, Tamara. *Squirrels of the West.* Vancouver, BC: Lone Pine, 1999.

Steele, Michael A., and John L. Koprowski. *North American Tree Squirrels.* Washington, DC: Smithsonian, 2003.

Thorington, Richard W. Jr., and Katie Ferrell. *Squirrels: The Animal Answer Guide.* Baltimore, MD: Johns Hopkins University Press, 2006.

To learn about squirrels and share your squirrel observations as part of a citizen science project, check out projectsquirrel.org.

Students who want to dig deeper into squirrel biology and environmental issues may want to study these squirrels in the news:

- The Delmarva fox squirrel is a subspecies of fox squirrel that is endangered. It lives on Virginia's and Maryland's eastern shores.
- In Britain, the Eurasian red squirrel is becoming rare because of habitat loss and competition with eastern gray squirrels brought from the United States.
- The western gray squirrel is listed as a threatened species in Washington State.